For larger orders of books, author's visits, and more information about this interdisciplinary series visit www.ArtsKindred.com
follow IG @ArtsKindred

Written by: Anetta Kotowicz
Illustrated by: Nina Ezhik
Graphic Concept and Art Direction by: Anetta Kotowicz

New York - 2018
Library of Congress Control Number: 2018907334

Hardcover ISBN: 978-1-7321862-3-1
Paperback ISBN: 978-1-7321862-9-3

This is NOT a typical picture book, it's much more!
Here's your guide to the interactive reading experience:

 Subscribe to Arts Kindred on YouTube to see crafts and listen to the music from this book. Select the Winter Song playlist. Scan the QR Code with your phone to do it now.

SCAN ME

Requires QR Code Reader App and Internet Connection

Pages marked with this symbol turn into songs when used with the Arts Kindred Magic app (Google Play Store users only).
Select the Winter Song book on the app's intro screen, and scan the spread with this symbol. You'll hear the songs, music, learn the sounds, and patterns of selected musical instruments used in this book. Depending on the compatibility of your device, you'll be surprised with 4D Augmented Reality experience - some characters may even magically come to life right in front of you in simplistic animations!
(Kids love this magic, adult's help and good lighting conditions required)
If your device is not compatible, you'll find the songs on the above mentioned YouTube channel!

Follow @ArtsKindred on Instagram for updates, activities, and announcements about other books and freebies.

CHECK OUT THIS WINTER LANTERN CRAFT #ArtsKindred

Our books are designed as a cohesive music-movement-art-nature provocation. Read them in sections, giving children opportunity to react, look and listen. Engage them into conversations, asking:
What do you hear when looking at that picture? Can you make this sound?
What else can you see, hear, and notice? How would this sound? What will happen next?

Listen to the songs, move to the music. Find sound-making objects at your home and improvise music with us. Paint a picture, make some crafts, sing a song, play a game, go on the nature walk, and show us what you've found.
Please share it with us #ArtsKindred.

For more information, conference presentations, interactive author's visits, and lessons contact us through **www.ArtsKindred.com**

To my Miko with Love
A.K.

A Day in the Life of a Kid:

WiNteR SonG

written by Anetta Kotowicz
illustrated by Nina Ezhik

artsKiNDRe♪
2018 New York

Every season has music
Every season shares joy
Every season sounds with colors

Can you hear it?
It's time to explore!

Good morning, Billy Bear,
Are you ready for a walk?
Let's find out what is waiting
For us, right there - outside!

It is cloudy, it is cold,
Our home is cozy and warm!
We are waiting patiently,
The magic will start soon...

Get your sweater and your snow pants,
Take your mittens, scarf, and hat,
Warmest jacket and big snow boots,
Winter's cold - We all know that!

Come outside and play with me today,
Come outside and play with me!
Winter has a **magic charm**,
We will have a joyful time.

Look and listen! It's so silent...
Tiny snowflakes fall around,

Whirling, twirling

very lightly,

'Till they gently

touch the ground.

Lightly **whirl and twirl**,
Sing a joyful Ding-Dong-Ding!
Lightly **whirl and twirl**,
Let the winter season sing!

Snowballs falling **POP-POP! POP-POP!**
Snowball fight! Get ready, start!
Make a snowball, toss it far,
It must reach the other side!

POP-POP! POP-POP! Whirl and twirl,
Sing a joyful Ding-Dong-Ding!
POP-POP! POP-POP! Whirl and twirl,
Let the winter season sing!

Look and listen!

Hear the sparkle,
Pointy icicles play along!
Winter sun rays magic music:
Ding-dong,
Ding-dong,
Ding-Dong Song!

DING-DONG!
Whirl and twirl,
Sing a joyful Ding-Dong-Ding!
DING-DONG!
Whirl and twirl,
Let the winter season sing!

Time to   walk with   friends to - ge - ther

stomp   stomp   stomp stomp   stomp stomp stomp   stomp

Throw some   snowballs   in such   weather

pop-pop   pop-pop   pop-pop   pop-pop

Roll   a   big one,   medium,   small

Ro - o - o - oll   Roll

Watch the   snowman   growing   tall!

Is that all?
Oh, no!

Look and listen!
Winter's calling:
Horses pull the **jingling** sled!
Hear the smiles and joyful voices,
Winter music in my head!

Look and listen!
Winter's calling
Be my helpers, everyone!
Bake the cookies, set the tables,
Share the stories
from near and far!

Look up now! On the snowy tree,
A few little red birds
Are chirping at me:

Chirp-chirp, chirp-chirp,
We have some hungry bellies,
Chirp-chirp, chirp-chirp,
No seeds, no yummy berries!

Don't forget to feed us
In the winter time,
And we will sing a song for you
When **spring** will come!

In the silence of a snowy day,
Trees and buildings, stars above,
Brilliant lights shine all around,
Spreading kindness, peace and love!

Candlelight,
shining bright,
Sparkling peaceful light,

Candlelight,
shining bright,
Warming every heart,

Stars above,
help me shine,
just like the

Candlelight,
shining bright...

Party time!

We share our cookies,
Sip delicious hot cocoa,
Looking at the whisper
of the snow
We sing the winter's song.

What song?

Lightly whirl and twirl,
Sing a joyful **Ding-Dong-Ding!**
Lightly whirl and twirl,
Let the **winter season sing!**

Would you like to play games?

Flip this page...

SURPRISE!

Let's play!

Note about the board game:
- the best way to play is by enlarging it
- game instructions on the last page of the book

LOOK:

Find these crafts in our book, just flip the pages and look again.
Make your own crafts - inspirations @ArtsKindred

*slices of dried oranges, pinecones, anise stars, cinnamon sticks
cranberries or popcorn on the strings, make great smelling ornaments*

*make festive chains with your drawings
on colored paper and attach them to
the string or ribbon*

*simple lantern,
made by decorating
a glass jar*

*bird friendly feeder - like this,
holding seeds mixed with a touch
of oil, made of an orange peel*

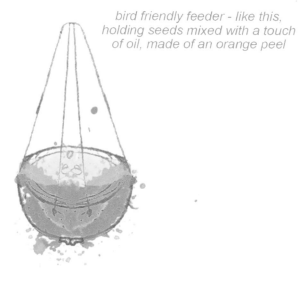

LISTEN:

Find the Winter Song playlist on the ArtsKindred YouTube channel, and listen to the chant called the Winter Music.

Look at the pictures below. Can you name all the instruments? Where is the jingle bell, triangle, tambourine, chimes bar, glockenspiel, bongos and big cymbals?

Download the Arts Kindred Magic app to learn the sounds of these instruments, and play with songs and rhythm patterns.

Are you ready for your winter music and craft party, or a dance? Let us see your ideas! Follow IG @ArtsKindred and post #ArtsKindred

WINTER

is a wonderful time for listening to the stories from other cultures and countries. We can learn and share many traditions, customs, and songs, just check the traditional European cakes and cookies in our book!

We also like making outdoor decorations that birds and wildlife will enjoy. Later we can observe lots of prints in the snow and learn who visited us. How do you like to spend long winter's evenings?

HI! It's me, Pompon!

Did you read my Autumn Song? I hope you didn't miss it! I had so much fun exploring the autumn season. Can't wait to do it again with you!

WinteR SonG

SNOW PRINTS GAME
music and movement board game

On the other side of this page is a board game to play with friends and family!

How to use it?

1. You may play it As Is - right on the book

2. Cut out both game pages from the book, as close as possible to the center of the book (spine), and use scotch tape to connect both pages. To make it more studry, you may glue the pages on a larger piece of cardboard and decorate it.

Enjoy the fun time!

0

41

42

43
sleep 1 turn

44

45

Finish

Start

1

2

3

4

5

6

7

8

9

Climbing, climbing up the hill

Let's slide down on our backs!

Wheeee!

The ride goes   smooth and fast -

THUMP!

Can you   follow snowy tracks?

16

15

14

13

12

11

10

It's time for your happy dance!
Let us see it   #ArtsKindred

WINTER GAME INSTRUCTIONS:

You need 1 pawn for each player and 1 die to share when taking turns,
or be creative and substitute these with easy-to-find objects - it's up to you!
(Ex. a die - you write numbers on a rubber eraser side,
as a pawn - use some small figures or blocks in different colors)

You'll also need an instrument - a bell. Don't worry if you don't have it!
How about finding something that makes the "right sound"?
Just look around - empty pots, metal bowls or buckets, some wooden spoons,
pot lids, they all work great!

Here is our bell - the jingle bell, but all bells are great!
Another choice: use our app to make sounds, but it's more fun with real instruments!

Start. Roll a die and move your pawn. Look where you landed.
Space with the bell? Make a bell concert and sing along if you like.
Space with animal tracks? Guess who left those tracks in the snow and move
around the room like your animal:

rabbit: reindeer: bird:

Don't forget to have a dance party on the finish line - and some snacks too!

ENJOY THE GAME!

Hi kids and adults!

Thank you for purchasing my book. My friends in A Day In A Life Of A Kid series and I would like to hear from you! We love receiving letters and seeing your crafts, dances, nature walks, and music activities. You can share them with us on Instagram or Facebook pages using #ArtsKindred and follow us @artskindred. Find additional music and art activities on www.ArtsKindred.com, and subscribe to the ArtsKindred YouTube channel.

Please help other readers find out about our books, and consider leaving an Amazon review if your child/students enjoyed interacting with us.

Thank you,
Anetta Kotowicz

Find more Creative and Interdisciplinary Curriculum books
by visiting www.ArtsKindred.com
or by typing ArtsKindred into the Amazon search box.

CPSIA information can be obtained
at www.ICGtesting.com
Printed in the USA
LVHW072346161221
706446LV00014B/46